10°-MINUTE DEVOTIONS
FOR YOUTH GROUPS

By J.B. Collingsworth

Group® Books

Loveland, Colorado

10-Minute Devotions for Youth Groups

Copyright © 1989 by J.B. Collingsworth

Third printing, 1990

Credits
Edited by Cindy Hansen
Designed by Judy Atwood Bienick

Scripture quotations are from the Holy Bible, New International Version. Copyright © 1973, 1978, 1984 International Bible Society. Used by permission of Zondervan Bible Publishers.

Library of Congress Cataloging-in-Publication Data
Collingsworth, J.B.
    10-minute devotions for youth groups.

    Includes index.
    1. Youth—Prayer-books and devotions—English.
I. Title.   II. Title: Ten-minute devotions for youth groups.
BV4850.C566   1989   242'.63   89-7576
ISBN 0-931529-85-9

Printed in the United States of America

Dedication

To the memory of my parents, Joe and Justine Collingsworth, whose unconditional love gave me the courage to seek the best in life. Special gratitude is expressed to God for the spiritual foundation my mother laid.

To my wife, Anne Leavell (Shugie) Collingsworth, for her love, prayer, support and encouragement every day that I live.

To my children, Mary Margaret, Robert Leavell and Wesley Joseph, whose lives add that special sparkle that makes life so very special.

To my sisters (and their families), Jean Cole and Judy Laird, for their years of loving concern for their little brother.

To my sister, JoAnn Bosworth, and her family for just being there.

To my in-laws, Bobby and Margaret Mann, whose love and acceptance as a part of their family has made me value their wisdom and council.

Acknowledgments

I would like to offer special thanks to Julie Davis, my secretary, and to Julie Cole, my niece, for their help in typing (and retyping) the manuscript for this book.

A special thank you to all the pastors, churches and youth groups I have served. They have been instrumental as the proving ground for what is contained in this book. Special thanks to O.D. Oliver, Rod Masteller and James W. Bryant.

A special thank you to the Louisiana Baptist Convention for allowing me to tackle this project, and to Group Books for asking me to write it and for encouraging me along the way.

Contents

10-MINUTE Devotions on Faith Issues

10°-MINUTE Devotions for Special Occasions

Introduction

10-Minute Devotions for Youth Groups is filled with devotions that can be used at a campout, at a retreat, at the beginning of a Bible study, right before a speaker, right after a powerful movie—whenever you need to introduce a topic or cement a lesson that's been taught. The creative devotions are based on a variety of scripture and a variety of themes.

DEVOTION ELEMENTS

Each devotion consists of the following seven elements.

Theme: This is the topic of the devotion, the main thought. Themes cover a variety of teenagers' needs and concerns.

Scripture: Each devotion is based on scripture that supports the theme and shows kids that God is concerned about every area of their lives.

Overview: This brief statement describes the devotion and tells what the participants will learn.

Preparation: This part describes exactly what materials you'll need for the devotion and what you'll need to do to prepare for it.

When preparing for the devotions, remember to involve the young people themselves. They can help round up supplies, but they can also help lead. The devotions are easy-to-follow and easy-to-prepare. Even busy teenagers can find time to prepare and lead these quick devotions. Involving teenagers as much as possible gives them ownership of the devotion and helps them develop leadership skills they will keep their whole lives.

Experience: Each devotion contains a unique element that lets kids actually experience the theme. Kids use their senses of sight, hearing, smell, touch and taste to gain a deeper understanding of the topic being discussed.

All activities can be adapted to fit the size of your group. If you have a small group, simply do the devotional activities together. If you have a larger group, divide into small groups using a variety of methods. For example, you can divide into small groups by eye color, hair color or birthdays. Or you can spell the theme for the devotion. If the theme is "Love," have the group members sound off by spelling "L-O-V-E." All "L's" form one group, all "O's" form another group, and so on.

■ **Response:** Participants take the experience one step further and think about what they've experienced and how it applies to their lives. They think about and discuss their discoveries.

■ **Closing:** Each devotion concludes with a prayer or activity that summarizes the devotional thought and helps kids apply it to their lives.

▩ *THE FOUR SECTIONS*

The devotions in this book are divided into four sections for easy reference. Here are the sections:

⏱ ● **10-Minute Devotions on Personal Spiritual Growth**—Some of the themes in this section are busyness, self-image, thankfulness, death, priorities and making a difference.

⏱ ● **10-Minute Devotions on Christ-Centered Relationships**—Themes in this section range from friendships and family relationships to relationships with the world. Kids discuss loyalty, encouragement, servanthood, gossip, God's love and unconditional acceptance.

⏱ ● **10-Minute Devotions on Faith Issues**—Themes in this section include sin, temptation, forgiveness, witnessing, commitment, faith and service.

⏱ ● **10-Minute Devotions for Special Occasions**—Themes in this section cover special days such as New Year's Day, Valentine's Day, Mother's Day, Father's Day, Easter, Thanksgiving, Christmas and school holidays.

Be sure to look through the themes in this section. Some of the devotions can be used throughout the year and not just for special occasions. For example, "Who Do We Appreciate?" on page 77 can be used for Mother's Day, Father's Day or for a parent-appreciation night. "Onward Toward the Goal" on page 79 can be used for graduation or any time during the year to emphasize keeping our eyes focused on God.

Be creative and have fun when you use *10-Minute Devotions for Youth Groups*. Adapt and use the quick devotions wherever and whenever you want.

10-MINUTE DEVOTIONS

on

Personal Spiritual Growth

All God's Blessings

■ **Theme:** Past, present, future blessings; thankfulness
■ **Scripture:** Genesis 13:14-16; Ezekiel 34:26
■ **Overview:** Young people will play a game, discuss past, present and future blessings, and learn how to respond.
■ **Preparation:** Gather several pieces of paper and newsprint, pencils and markers. You'll also need a Bible.

✎EXPERIENCE

Have the kids form a line. Have the first kid in line say, "Past"; the next kid say, "Present"; and the third kid say, "Future." Then start with "Past" again. Continue this pattern down the line. Divide into three groups with all the "Pasts" forming one group, and so on. If you have a small group, play the game individually. Give each group a piece of paper and newsprint, pencil and marker. On its paper, have each group list five things group members think are blessings from God. The blessings could be from the past (a good friend in grade school), present (a good family) or future (a healthy lifestyle). Have groups discuss their choices.

Have each group share its list of five blessings by drawing them, one at a time, on newsprint. Instruct the other two groups to try to guess the blessing. When a group guesses the proper answer, it receives one point.

◈RESPONSE

As the teams draw their lists of blessings, compile a master list of blessings on a separate piece of newsprint. When the game is completed, read aloud Genesis 13:14-16 and Ezekiel 34:26. Talk about how God abundantly blesses his people. Discuss how to respond to God's blessings.

✎CLOSING

Close with prayer in the small groups. Encourage each group to thank God for the blessings on its list. ■

Biting Bitterness

■ **Theme:** Bitterness, resentment, anger
■ **Scripture:** Ephesians 4:31-32
■ **Overview:** Group members tangle themselves up in yarn and learn that bitterness, resentment and anger can cause all kinds of problems.
■ **Preparation:** You'll need a Bible and a ball of yarn.

◈EXPERIENCE

To illustrate the fact that bitterness, resentment and anger can cause all kinds of problems, tangle the group in yarn. You start first. Wrap yarn around your waist and say: Bitterness, resentment, anger.

Toss the ball of yarn to another who repeats the process. Continue until each person is tangled in the yarn of "bitterness, resentment and anger."

◈RESPONSE

As you are tied up in knots discuss: What tangled feelings come with bitterness, resentment and anger? What causes these feelings?

Read aloud Ephesians 4:31-32 and have the group members untangle themselves. Ask: How can we untangle feelings of bitterness, resentment and anger?

◈CLOSING

Ask everyone to hold on to the tangled mass of yarn. Pray: God, untangle our tangled feelings of bitterness, resentment and anger. Help us to love those who hurt us and be kind to those who anger us. Amen. ■

Cut the Clutter

■ **Theme:** Cluttered lives

■ **Scripture:** Philippians 4:8

■ **Overview:** Group members each will think about the clutter of objects and events in their life and decide what one thing they want to do to simplify their lifestyle.

■ **Preparation:** Stuff a paper sack with items that could be found in a school locker, such as candy wrappers, books, soft drink cans, pencils, tennis shoes, socks, lunch sacks, and so on. You'll also need a Bible.

EXPERIENCE

Gather the group members in a circle, and pull items from the sack as you talk. Say: This sack of stuff could have come from one of your lockers. Some things were good once, but aren't now. Some are still good.

Ask a person to read aloud Philippians 4:8. Talk about how our lives are to be full of the excellent, good things that are right, pure and lovely.

RESPONSE

Ask the young people each to think about something they want to unclutter from their life. Pass around the sack and ask each person to take out something that symbolizes that clutter. For example, a person could take out a tennis shoe to represent the desire to cut out all the unnecessary "running around" and to take time for quiet. Have kids each discuss their selected item and how they plan to remove the clutter from their life.

CLOSING

Step on a soft drink can from the sack. Say: This can can be recycled and salvaged, just as God can or has recycled our lives through his Son. God helps us cut out the clutter. He helps us become totally new through Christ. ■

Delegate!

■ **Theme:** Busyness

■ **Scripture:** Exodus 18:17-24

■ **Overview:** Group members will use balloons to illustrate the topic of busyness and will examine the need to delegate.

■ **Preparation:** Gather one inflated balloon for each person. Ask one young person to study the devotion in advance and volunteer every time you ask for help. You'll also need a Bible.

▩ EXPERIENCE

After everyone is gathered, ask for volunteers for a variety of tasks. For example: I need someone to teach a Bible study. I need someone to mow the grass. I need someone to visit the nursing home residents. I need someone to make posters. I need someone to fix the door in the youth room. And I need someone to do a radio spot for the big concert.

One young person volunteers to do it all. As that person volunteers for each task, toss him or her an inflated balloon. The volunteer will soon realize he or she can't do everything (especially juggle all of those inflated balloons).

Have someone read aloud Exodus 18:17-24, where Jethro tells Moses to learn to delegate responsibility and teach others how to help.

▩ RESPONSE

The volunteer gets the idea and begins distributing the balloons to other people who can help. The volunteer briefly explains what to do. For example, "You can help lead a Bible study. You can mow the grass. You can visit the nursing home. You can help make posters." The volunteer distributes the balloons and tasks.

Say: Do you get the idea? One person can't do everything and do it well. We all can help because we all are capable. So let's remember to delegate.

Emphasize this point by playing a few minutes of "Balloon Delegation." Distribute balloons to everyone. Encourage the young people to bat their balloons in the air and try to keep them from touching the ground. On the word "Delegate," they each bat their balloon to someone else and bat a different balloon. Try "delegating" a few times. Ask the players to hold their balloons for the prayer.

CLOSING

Pray: God, help us to not be so busy doing good that we fail to involve others. Help us not hesitate to delegate.

On the word "Amen," have all group members pop their balloons. ∎

First Things First

■ **Theme:** Priorities
■ **Scripture:** Matthew 6:31-33; 1 John 2:15
■ **Overview:** Group members take time to think about important things in their lives.
■ **Preparation:** Gather newsprint, a marker and a Bible. Each person will need a pencil and a "Priorities" handout.

▦EXPERIENCE

Give the group members each a pencil and a "Priorities" handout. Ask them each to list the top five priorities in their life right now. For example, a #1 priority could be time with friends, a #2 priority could be eating right, and so on. Tell kids their answers will be discussed in an anonymous way, so they can be completely honest.

▦RESPONSE

Collect all of the #5 priorities by having group members tear off their #5 answers along the dotted line. With a marker, list their answers on the piece of newsprint. Do the same with numbers four, three, two and one.

Ask a young person to read aloud Matthew 6:31-32 and 1 John 2:15. Ask kids to assess their priorities according to what the Bible verses say. Ask: What are the majority of #1 priorities? According to the Bible verses, what should be our #1 priority? How can we make Christ our #1 priority?

▦CLOSING

Read Matthew 6:33 aloud together: "But seek first his kingdom and his righteousness, and all these things will be given to you as well." Have kids each hold up their right pointer finger and say, "Christ is #1 in my life." ■

Priorities

Instructions: List the top five priorities in your life right now.

1.

2.

3.

4.

5.

Never Alone

- **Theme:** Failure
- **Scripture:** Exodus 4:10-13; Nehemiah 4:10-23
- **Overview:** Group members will have a "moving" experience with failure and will understand that God is always with them.
- **Preparation:** Find a large object that can't be moved by one person. For example, a piano, boulder or small car.

⊕EXPERIENCE

Meet by the large object. One at a time, have individuals try to move it. After all of the failed attempts, have the whole group move it together.

⊕RESPONSE

Say: We all fail and become discouraged at one time or another. There are things that no one can do alone.

Ask a volunteer to read aloud Exodus 4:10-13. Discuss how Moses thought he couldn't do what God wanted, but *with* God he did great things.

Then ask a volunteer to read aloud Nehemiah 4:10-23. Discuss how the Jews worked together to rebuild the wall. They couldn't do it alone. They needed each other.

⊕CLOSING

Ask everyone to stand with their hands to their sides. Pray: God, be with us when we try things by ourselves and fail.

Ask kids to form a giant chain by joining hands. Then pray: God, help us to join forces and not be defeated. Through Christ we can do all things. Amen. ■

One Life to Live

///

■ **Theme:** Death
■ **Scripture:** Revelation 2:10b
■ **Overview:** Death is a topic we avoid, especially in this busy, hectic life. Use this devotion to slow everyone down and give kids each time to reflect on their life.
■ **Preparation:** Gather a Bible and several obituaries from a distant city's newspaper. Each person will need one piece of chalk. Be sure it's okay to write on the sidewalk with chalk. Part of this devotion will be held outside. If it's too cold, meet inside and supply a sheet of newsprint and a marker for each person.

✏EXPERIENCE

Divide your kids into groups of two or three. Distribute the obituaries so that each group has one. Give the kids time to summarize the life of the person in their obituary, as if they were going to inscribe a few sentences on his or her tombstone. For example, "Here lies John Smith. Beloved husband. Beloved father. Dedicated church member." After a few minutes, have each group share its inscriptions.

◊RESPONSE

Lead the young people to the sidewalk outside. Give each person a piece of chalk. If it is too cold, do this activity inside with the newsprint and marker. Tell the kids to think of how they want to be remembered for the life they live. Have them each design and draw a tombstone and inscription on the sidewalk or on the newsprint. After a few minutes, have the kids describe their tombstone inscriptions.

◊CLOSING

Read Revelation 2:10b aloud. Remind the kids they have only one life to live. Close with a prayer asking God's help to live so that others will see Christ in each person. ■

Salty Characters

■ **Theme:** Making a difference
■ **Scripture:** Matthew 5:13
■ **Overview:** Everyone can make a difference in this world. This devotion gives group members a "taste" for that topic.
■ **Preparation:** Gather a Bible, a bowl of salt-free peanuts and a bowl of salty peanuts. You'll also need one small packet of salty peanuts for each person.

EXPERIENCE

Gather kids in a circle. Then pass the bowl of salt-free peanuts. Ask everyone to take one and eat it. Read Matthew 5:13 aloud. Then pass the bowl of salty peanuts. Again, ask everyone to take one and eat it.

RESPONSE

Discuss the following questions: Describe the difference between the two kinds of peanuts. Which did you like best? Why? How is the salt-free peanut like living a bland life? Why doesn't Jesus want his children to be bland? Why are we expected to add salt to the world? What does that mean?

CLOSING

Pass the bowl of salty peanuts and let kids crunch as you pray aloud: Lord, help us to be salt that flavors the world. May our friends want what we have because they see flavor in our lives that reflects you. Amen.

Give the kids each a packet of salty peanuts to take home. Have them eat the peanuts later to serve as reminders to be salt to the world. ■

Temper, Temper

- **Theme:** Anger
- **Scripture:** Colossians 3:8; Ephesians 4:26-27
- **Overview:** In this devotion kids will develop some dos and don'ts for dealing with anger.
- **Preparation:** Gather a Bible, some newsprint and a marker. Make up a monologue in which you yell about someone who's mistreated you.

EXPERIENCE

Walk into the room and begin yelling in anger. Shout about someone who's mistreated you. For example: I can't believe it. After all I've done for my friend. I've loaned her money when she's needed it. I've loaned her a car when she's needed it. I've loaned her a listening ear whenever she's needed it. And do you think she'd listen to me? No! She ran away from home.

While you are still boiling with anger, have someone read aloud Colossians 3:8 and Ephesians 4:26-27. Then ask the group members what the verses say about how you should handle your anger.

RESPONSE

Using members' suggestions, create a list of dos and don'ts for handling anger. A don't could be "Don't hit others." A do could be "Do deal with your anger in a positive way, like taking a walk to cool down."

CLOSING

Close with a group prayer where each person can add a sentence by using one of the dos or don'ts from the list. For example: Dear God, help us to deal with our anger in a positive way. Help us to not hit or hurt another when we are angry. ■

Time Flies

■ **Theme:** Changes, wishes

■ **Scripture:** Ecclesiastes 3:1-8

■ **Overview:** Group members will go through a "time machine" and think of things they want to change now.

■ **Preparation:** Find an empty refrigerator box at an appliance store. Cut out one side of it for a doorway. On the front, use a marker or paintbrush to write "Time Machine." Get all the ingredients you need to make and eat banana splits. You'll also need a Bible.

EXPERIENCE

After everyone is gathered in the room, show them the time machine and say: I'll give you 30 seconds to think of a time you'd like to go back to and a change you'd like to make. For example, you could want to go back to the beginning of a war and help the countries talk about rather than fight over their problems.

One at a time let kids say what time they'd go back to and what they'd change. Go into the time machine (knock around in it as if it's working), and then step out.

RESPONSE

After everyone has had a turn in the time machine, read Ecclesiastes 3:1-8 aloud. Say: Notice. Everyone went through the time machine but nothing changed. We can't change the past. Let's focus on how we can make a difference today and in the future.

CLOSING

Show everyone the supplies to make banana splits. Tell kids this is a "timed" race. Every second counts. The last two finished creating their banana splits will have to clean up. Get the banana split sculptors going by saying: On your mark, get set, go! ■

Who's the Fairest?

- **Theme:** Self-image
- **Scripture:** 1 Corinthians 6:19-20
- **Overview:** Kids will reflect about their good qualities.
- **Preparation:** Gather a "Mirror, Mirror" handout and a pencil for each person. You also will need a Bible and a mirror.

EXPERIENCE

Pass around a mirror. Instruct the young people to each look at their reflection and think about five things they like about themselves.

Distribute the "Mirror, Mirror" handout and pencils. Tell the kids to each write the five things they like about themselves. Tell them they can write anything they want because no one will see their answers. When the kids finish, have them fold their papers and keep them for reference during the week.

RESPONSE

Read aloud 1 Corinthians 6:19-20 and discuss the following questions: What does it mean to be the temple of the Holy Spirit? What does it mean to be bought at a price? What does it mean to honor God with our bodies? How can you reflect God's love through your actions?

CLOSING

Ask everyone to turn to the person standing closest to him or her. Have the pairs face each other and play the game "Mirrors." One partner initiates actions and the other reflects or imitates the actions. Then have them switch.

Close by having the partners hold hands. Pray: God, thank you for making us just as we are. Help us to look in the mirror and like what we see and who we are. Help us reflect your love through our actions. Amen. ■

Mirror, Mirror

Instructions: "Mirror, mirror on the wall . . . who's the fairest of them all?" According to God, you are the fairest of them all. He loves you so much he gave his Son to die for your sins. Reflect about your good qualities.

List five things you like about yourself. For example, your smile, your eyes, your willingness to listen. Keep the paper and reread it during the week. Remember that God loves you.

Five things I like about me:

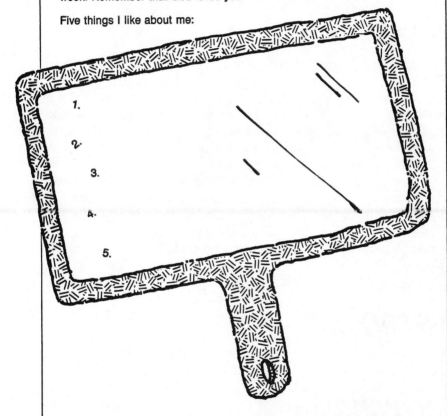

1.

2.

3.

4.

5.

"Do you not know that your body is a temple of the Holy Spirit, who is in you, whom you have received from God? You are not your own; you were bought at a price. Therefore honor God with your body" (1 Corinthians 6:19-20).

Worrywarts

- **Theme:** Worry, anxiety
- **Scripture:** Luke 12:22-31
- **Overview:** Partners will symbolize worry and God's wish that we forget our anxieties.
- **Preparation:** You'll need a Bible.

EXPERIENCE

Divide the group into pairs by having kids each find a person with the same-color eyes. Tell partners that one is the sculptor and the other is the clay. The sculptors make a statue to symbolize a person who is weighed down by worries. For example, the statue could look as if he or she is straining to support a huge weight on his or her back. Have an art show of the various creations.

Read aloud Luke 12:22-31. Then switch: the sculptors are now clay and the statues are now sculptors. Say: Sculptors, form a statue to symbolize Christ shouldering all our cares and anxieties. We have nothing to worry about. For example, the statue could smile and raise his or her arms in the air.

Have another art show with these creations.

RESPONSE

Talk about some of the worries kids have. Ask why it is sometimes easier to worry than offer our cares to God.

CLOSING

Encourage the kids to silently offer their worries to God as you pray: God, hear each of the worries we offer silently to you now . . . (pause). Forgive us for worrying. Help us trust you. We know you care what happens to us. You love us above all things. Amen. ■

10-MINUTE DEVOTIONS

on

Christ-Centered Relationships

Accept Me, Please

■ **Theme:** Rejection
■ **Scripture:** Isaiah 41:9; 1 Timothy 4:4
■ **Overview:** Group members will feel rejection and acceptance in this devotion.
■ **Preparation:** You'll need one sheet of paper for each person. On half of the pieces of paper write "Reject me"; on the other pieces of paper write "Smile at me and accept me." You'll also need a Bible and some tape.

✎EXPERIENCE

Tell kids: I'm going to tape a piece of paper to each of your backs. The paper tells others how to treat you. On the word "Go," mingle and treat each other as the signs on your backs indicate.

After a few minutes, read aloud Isaiah 41:9 and 1 Timothy 4:4.

◈RESPONSE

Discuss the following questions: How did it feel to be rejected? accepted? How did it feel to reject another? accept another? When was the last time you rejected someone at school? home? church?

✎CLOSING

Gather the kids in a circle with their backs toward the center. Pray: God, help us not reject others, because we know what it feels like to be rejected—not good.

Have kids turn to face the center and put their arms around each other. Pray: God, help us to love and accept each other as you love and accept us. Amen. ■

Broken Families

■ **Theme:** Divorce, healing

■ **Scripture:** Psalm 34:18; 147:3

■ **Overview:** Group members reflect on their views of divorce and healing.

■ **Preparation:** You'll need a Bible, "Questions About Divorce" handout and pencil for each person. You will also need a marker and some newsprint.

EXPERIENCE

Ask all the guys to interlock arms and form a circle. Tell the girls they have 30 seconds to try to break the guys' circle. Then switch. Have the girls form a circle and let the guys try to break it. Say: Divorce is breaking a relationship. Two people, a family, interlocked over the years, being broken apart.

RESPONSE

Give each person a "Questions About Divorce" handout, Bible and pencil. Have the kids answer the questions. Then have kids pair up and discuss their answers. After the discussion have partners share one discovery or question with the whole group. Then say: Divorce affects all of our lives. Our parents may be divorced, someone in our family may be divorced or we may have friends who come from a divorced home. What are some ideas for healing the brokenness and hurt when divorce occurs?

Write the ideas on the newsprint.

CLOSING

Have guys and girls form one large circle by interlocking arms. Pray: God, comfort and be near those who have experienced a broken relationship. As you promised in the psalm, "Heal the brokenhearted and bind up their wounds." Amen. ■

Questions About Divorce

Instructions: Answer these questions about divorce. Then discuss them with a partner.

 1. What are some causes for divorce?

 2. Who feels guilty when a divorce occurs?

 3. How does a divorce affect children of the family?

 4. What are ways to heal the brokenness that occurs during a divorce?

 5. What do Psalms 34:18; and 147:3 say about healing?

Brotherly Love

■ **Theme:** Brothers and sisters
■ **Scripture:** 1 Timothy 5:1-2
■ **Overview:** Group members will learn to be sensitive to siblings.
■ **Preparation:** You'll need a Bible and aluminum foil.

EXPERIENCE

Divide the group into small groups by having them count off from one to five. All ones form a group, all twos form a group, and so on. Give each group a piece of aluminum foil and tell each of them one of these "lines" you might hear a brother or sister say:

- "Get out of the bathroom."
- "Would you hurry up? The phone is for you."
- "Don't snoop in my room."
- "It's your turn to wash the dishes, not mine."
- "Wait until Mom (or Dad) gets home. You're in trouble."

Have the groups form an aluminum shape to symbolize their "line." For example, a group could shape a phone receiver to symbolize "Would you hurry up? The phone is for you."

RESPONSE

Discuss the lines brothers and sisters sometimes exchange and the groups' symbols for those lines. Read aloud 1 Timothy 5:1-2, then ask: How do siblings usually treat each other? According to the passage, how should siblings treat each other? Why is it sometimes difficult to be nice to a brother or sister? Some brothers and sisters have no trouble being nice to each other. How do they do it? How can we treat our siblings as friends?

▨ CLOSING

Put all the aluminum shapes in the middle of the room. Have the members form a circle around the objects and join hands for a closing prayer. You lead the prayer and ask God for patience and love when it comes to dealing with siblings. ■

Clones

■ **Theme:** Peer pressure

■ **Scripture:** Genesis 37:5-24

■ **Overview:** Group members will see before their very eyes the effects of peer pressure on normal human beings.

■ **Preparation:** Ask five young people to dress exactly alike. For example, they could wear blue jeans, white T-shirts and white tennis shoes. Have them prepare a silent skit where they all sit down the same, cross their legs the same, comb their hair the same, and so on. Instruct them to be prepared to read the scripture in a monotone voice. Bring five different articles of outer clothing such as a hat, scarf, jacket, gloves and belt.

EXPERIENCE

Having instructed them ahead of time, have the five young people come into the room without saying a word. Have them act out their skit.

RESPONSE

After the skit, ask the five "clones" to read the scripture, four verses per person. Have them read their verses in a monotone. Then discuss these questions: What are the drawbacks of looking the same or sounding the same as others? What are the good points? Is there safety in the feeling of "sameness"? Explain. How do your friends and peers influence you? How is this influence good? bad? How did peer pressure lead Joseph's brothers to do something bad? Could Reuben have stopped them if he wanted? Why didn't anyone try to stop them? Why should we try to be an individual and not go along with something we know is wrong? Why is this sometimes difficult?

CLOSING

Add some article of clothing to each of the five clones

to make them look different from each other. For example, place a hat on one person's head, wrap a scarf around the neck of another, and so on. Say: Each of us is created as a unique person. We need courage to celebrate our uniqueness. We need courage to withstand peer pressure. God gives us that courage. ■

Do What I Do

■ **Theme:** Leadership, peer pressure

■ **Scripture:** Ephesians 5:1; 1 John 2:1-6

■ **Overview:** Group members will follow the leader on an "imitation hike" to experience leadership and peer pressure.

■ **Preparation:** You'll need ingredients for ice cream sundaes, bowls, spoons and napkins. Set up an ice cream sundae assembly line for refreshment time.

▨ EXPERIENCE

Say: I am the leader. You must follow me and do exactly what I do.

Lead the others in activities such as crawling up stairs, skipping across a room and jogging in place. Have the members take turns leading and following.

◈ RESPONSE

Lead the others to form a circle. Ask two volunteers to read aloud Ephesians 5:1 and 1 John 2:1-6. Ask: What was it like to be a leader? a follower? How do you know if a leader is a good leader? How do you know if the leader wants you to do good or bad things? What are reasons to follow the right crowd? How do you know what is a right crowd? What are ways you can be good leaders to others? How can you imitate Christ?

▨ CLOSING

Play follow the leader again; this time you lead the group members to the ice cream sundae assembly line. Continue the discussion while munching the goodies. ■

Good, Bad, Rowdy

■ **Theme:** Unconditional acceptance
■ **Scripture:** Luke 15:11-32
■ **Overview:** Unconditional acceptance can be a rare thing today. Give kids a chance to experience it in this devotion.
■ **Preparation:** You'll need a piece of candy for each person, and a Bible.

EXPERIENCE

Divide the group in two by having kids one at a time say either, "Unconditional" or "Acceptance." Continue this pattern through all the kids. Have all "Unconditionals" form one group and all "Acceptances" form another.

Take one group aside and tell members they should be rowdy throughout the entire reading of the scripture. Gather the groups and read aloud Luke 15:11-32.

After the reading say: I have a reward for your behavior. Give everyone in both groups a piece of candy.

RESPONSE

Ask these questions: How did the "good" group feel when the "rowdy" group was rewarded in the same way? How was the good group similar to the oldest son in the passage? How was the rowdy group similar to the prodigal son? What emotions do you think the faithful brother experienced? Have you ever felt this way? If so, explain.

CLOSING

Have each member of the good group find a member of the rowdy group, face him or her and hold hands. Read each line of this prayer and ask the kids to repeat it.

Lord, help us to control our feelings of jealousy . . .
And feelings of envy . . .
Thank you for your unconditional acceptance of us . . .
No matter what we do . . .
You love us . . .
We love you . . .
Amen. ■

Heartfelt Words

//

- ■ **Theme:** Encouragement
- ■ **Scripture:** Proverbs 16:24
- ■ **Overview:** Everyone needs a daily dosage of affirmation and encouragement. Use this devotion time to give group members a dose of good feelings.
- ■ **Preparation:** Cut a large heart shape from an 8½ ×11 sheet of construction paper for each young person. You'll also need a crayon or marker for each person, some masking tape and a Bible.

⬦ *EXPERIENCE*

Tape a large paper heart to the back of each young person. On the word "Go," have kids mingle around the room and write on each person's paper heart affirming reasons why he or she is loved. For example, "You always think of the positive side of problems."

⬙ *RESPONSE*

Gather kids in a circle and ask a young person to read aloud Proverbs 16:24. Have the group members take off their paper hearts and read the encouraging words. Discuss these questions: How did you feel when you read what others wrote about you? Did this activity encourage you? Why or why not? What kinds of things can you do this week to encourage others? For example, write affirming notes or make unexpected phone calls.

⬙ *CLOSING*

Ask each young person to find the person closest to him or her for a prayer partner. Partners exchange hearts and take turns thanking God for the other partner using the partner's affirmation heart. For example: "Dear God, thanks for Chad and his easygoing personality. He brightens the room when he walks into it. Amen." ■

Love in Action

■ **Theme:** Servanthood

■ **Scripture:** 1 John 3:17

■ **Overview:** This devotion on servanthood could be combined with a visit to a nursing home.

■ **Preparation:** Ask someone to role play a homeless person. He can dress in tattered clothing and hold a paper sack filled with meager possessions. Plant the person close to a nursing home. Arrange for your group to visit the residents after you encounter this role-played homeless person. If you want this devotion to be a 10-minute one, simply plant the homeless person near your meeting area. You can plan to visit a nursing home later. You will also need a Bible.

EXPERIENCE

Point out the homeless person you have "planted." Start a conversation with him and possibly make introductions. Notice how your group members handle the encounter. Ask the person how your group can help him. Have him shrug his shoulders. See if any of the kids offer ideas of ways they can help.

RESPONSE

Unveil the true identity of the homeless person and have him share his feelings about the encounter. How did he feel to be reached out to or not reached out to?

Ask him to read aloud 1 John 3:17. Talk about love in action and how we can respond to those less fortunate than ourselves. Brainstorm ways to help. For example, collect money or food and donate it to a local homeless shelter.

CLOSING

Encourage kids to remember this devotion on love in action as they visit with the nursing home residents or as they encounter other people in stores or on the sidewalks. ■

Love One Another

■ **Theme:** Love
■ **Scripture:** 1 John 4:7-8
■ **Overview:** Group members will experience God's love and show their love for each other.
■ **Preparation:** Gather several Bibles and blank pieces of paper. You'll also need a pencil and a copy of the "Affirmation Ad" handout for each person.

EXPERIENCE

Gather the kids in a circle. Ask one person to read aloud 1 John 4:7-8. Say: These verses say it so simply. We can show God's love by caring for others.

Divide the group into four small groups by having them sound off by spelling "L-O-V-E." All "L's" form one group, all "O's" form another, and so on. Give each small group a piece of paper, a pencil and a Bible. Explain: On your paper, paraphrase the verses in your own words. A paraphrase could be "God loves us. We show his love through our love to others." After you paraphrase the verses, decide how you will act out your thoughts. For example, your group could have someone read the paraphrase as the rest of the group hold hands and form the shape of a heart.

Have each group act out its paraphrased verses for the other groups.

RESPONSE

Ask young people to each find a partner from one of the other small groups. Give each person an "Affirmation Ad." Ask kids each to think about qualities they appreciate in their partner. Then have them complete the ad.

CLOSING

Ask the partners to exchange their ads and read the affirming note. Have all the members gather in a circle and say, "Because God loves us, we love each other." Include everyone in a group hug and shout, "Amen!" ■

♡ Affirmation Ad ♡

In Christ I love _____
                            (Partner's name)

Because _____

_____

_____
                            (Your name)

Rumors Hurt

■ **Theme:** Gossip

■ **Scripture:** Exodus 32; Ephesians 4:29

■ **Overview:** Group members will perform skits that illustrate how gossip hurts.

■ **Preparation:** Photocopy the "Rampant Rumors" handout and cut apart the skits on the sheet. You'll need props for the skits (popcorn and anything else you want to use), a Bible and a table of refreshments. Place the table of refreshments at one end of the meeting room.

◈ EXPERIENCE

Divide the kids into three groups. Assign each group one of the skits from the "Rampant Rumors" handout. Allow a few minutes for them to prepare the skits then shout: Lights, camera, action!

Have groups perform their skits.

▨ RESPONSE

After the three skits, discuss these questions: What happened as a result of the rumor about Moses' desertion? How do you think Moses felt about the way people talked about him when he was gone? What happens as a result of rumors today? How does it feel to be gossipped about? How does it feel to gossip about somebody? What guidelines can you think of to stop rumors? Read aloud Ephesians 4:29. What guideline does this verse give us to stop rumors?

▨ CLOSING

Call everyone's attention to the table of refreshments at one end of the room. Then have everyone stand at the opposite end of the room. Ask kids to tell a guideline (or step), one at a time, for stomping out rumors. With each guideline, the young people all take two steps toward the refreshment table. For example, "Don't spread a rumor when you hear one." (Everyone takes two steps.) "Don't say anything you know might hurt someone." (Everyone takes two more steps.) Encourage the kids to exaggerate their steps by stomping. When everyone reaches the refreshment table, celebrate the steps toward stomping out rumors by eating the snacks. ■

Rampant Rumors

● Skit #1

Have a young person come in happily tossing the contents of a bag of popcorn all over the floor. (The popcorn represents rumors.) He can take some, hand some to people, whisper and walk away until he runs into a "friend" and tries to hide all the popcorn behind his back. The other person points at all the popcorn and confronts him with the fact that she knows he has been telling ugly rumors about her and that she wants it stopped. The young person confesses, asks for forgiveness and then says, "I'll go back and tell everyone what I said wasn't true."

While the young person is trying to correct what he's done, someone dressed in black goes around and picks up all of the popcorn except a few pieces. When the young person realizes it is impossible to take back all the rumors he has spread, he picks up one piece of popcorn and lowers and shakes his head in shame at what he has done.

● Skit #2

Three or four people stand in a straight line. The first person looks like he has a juicy bit of gossip. He whispers it to his neighbor. She looks shocked and surprised. She passes it on to the next person who acts shocked and surprised. She then passes it on to her neighbor. Continue this gossip until the last person starts to listen, then raises his hand to signal "Stop." This person says: "Stop gossip in its tracks. Gossip hurts."

● Skit #3

Read Exodus 32 about the people of Israel building a golden calf. Portray what the Israelites might have said when they thought Moses deserted them. For example, "That Moses. Who does he think he is? Taking a vacation on top of that mountain. He's deserting us, that thoughtless guy. Let's show him a thing or two. We don't need him. Let's pitch in all of our jewelry and make a golden calf."

Serve One Another

■ **Theme:** Servanthood

■ **Scripture:** John 13:5-9; Galatians 5:13

■ **Overview:** Group members will learn about true servanthood when they have a chance to serve and be served in this footwashing experience.

■ **Preparation:** Gather one basin of warm soapy water, a towel and a Bible. You'll also need a circle of chairs. Enlist one person ahead of time to begin the washing.

EXPERIENCE

Gather the group members in a circle. Instruct them to be seated and take off their socks and shoes. Have one person come in with a basin of warm soapy water and a large towel and begin washing one person's feet. When finished, have this "servant" say, "Go and serve one another in love." The first "servant" then sits down in the circle. The person whose feet were just washed is to wash his or her neighbor's feet and repeat the message. Continue this process until kids each have washed another person's feet and have had their feet washed.

RESPONSE

Read aloud John 13:5-9 and Galatians 5:13. Then, one at a time, have each young person define the word "serve." Have them discuss their feelings of having their feet washed and of washing another person's feet.

CLOSING

Invite the group members to put on their socks and shoes and think of ways to put their "feet" into some servanthood opportunities. For example, volunteer to teach a Sunday school class, offer to help a brother or sister with homework, or watch for new people at school and make them feel welcome. ■

Stand by a Friend

■ **Theme:** Friendship, loyalty

■ **Scripture:** John 12:1-8; 18:1-5

■ **Overview:** Friendship and loyalty are topics a young person deals with every day. Lead a devotion on these topics and let young people ask questions and share concerns.

■ **Preparation:** Gather a Bible, telephone, table and chair. Place the telephone on the table in front of the meeting area. Ask a young person to present a role play.

EXPERIENCE

Have a young person perform a role play. He enters the room, picks up the phone and talks to his friend who's in trouble. The young person is quick to tell his friend that he will stand by him no matter what.

A sample phone conversation could be:

"Hello? Oh, hello, Tom. What's the matter? Your English teacher thinks you cheated on the test? What happened? Oh, I'm sorry. I want you to know I'm here if you ever need to talk to someone."

RESPONSE

Put the phone conversation "on hold." Ask a young person to read aloud John 12:1-8. Then ask another young person to read aloud John 18:1-5. Discuss these questions: Would you stand by your friend regardless of the circumstance? Why or why not? Are there times when you can support a friend but not support the activity he or she is involved in? Explain. Why did Judas betray Jesus? Was it for personal gain? selfishness? ambition? Why didn't he stand by Jesus no matter what?

Give kids an opportunity to ask their own questions and voice their concerns about friendship and loyalty.

⊞ CLOSING

Ask everyone to stand in a circle around the telephone and hold hands. Pray: Lord, help us to stand by our friends when they're hurting or in trouble. Help us see beyond what our friends do, and love them as you love us. Thanks for standing by us whenever we call on you. Amen. ■

Violent World

▰▰▰▰▰▰▰▰▰▰▰▰▰▰▰▰▰▰▰▰▰▰▰▰▰▰▰▰▰▰▰▰▰▰▰▰▰▰▰

■ **Theme:** The world, violence, God's love
■ **Scripture:** Psalm 3:1-8; John 14:27
■ **Overview:** Young people will view news clips of violent happenings in the world and think about God's peace that passes all understanding.
■ **Preparation:** Videotape eight scenes of violence from the news. Get permission from the TV stations or networks to use the tape with your group. Bring the videotape and equipment to the devotion. You'll also need a Bible.

▧ EXPERIENCE

Show the first violent scene. Ask a young person to read Psalm 3:1. Show the second violent scene. Ask another young person to read Psalm 3:2. Continue this process until all eight scenes are shown and all eight verses of Psalm 3 are read.

▨ RESPONSE

Discuss these questions: What can violence do to people? What does Psalm 3:1-8 say about being troubled? How can we help keep peace? What does John 14:27 tell us about God's peace in a sometimes violent world?

◈ CLOSING

Close with a one-word prayer. Form a circle with the kids. You begin the prayer by saying: God hear us as we offer our concerns to you.

Then let each person offer a one-word concern brought up from the devotion. For example, peace, forgiveness, hurt, healing. End with: Thank you for hearing our prayers. Help us to know your peace that passes all understanding. Through your Son, Jesus. Amen. ■

10°-MINUTE DEVOTIONS
on
Faith Issues

A Balancing Act

■ **Theme:** Perspective

■ **Scripture:** Numbers 11:1-9

■ **Overview:** Kids will do an egg walk to illustrate the need for a proper perspective.

■ **Preparation:** Gather a dozen raw eggs, a piece of plastic sheeting (at least 6'×8'), a blindfold, a trash can and a Bible. Meet outside. Place the large piece of plastic on the ground. Then place the eggs around on the plastic.

EXPERIENCE

Gather the group members by the plastic you have prepared earlier. Then blindfold a volunteer. Divide the young people into two teams by having them count off in twos. All ones are the "helpers" group and they stand to the left of the plastic. All twos are the "distracters" group and they stand to the right of the plastic. Put the volunteer at one end and instruct him or her to walk where the helpers' team instructs.

The helpers want the volunteer to walk to the other end of the sheet without stepping on the eggs. The distracters shout and cheer and tell the volunteer directions that will make him or her step on the eggs. As the two teams shout orders, the volunteer will lose perspective and will inevitably step on some eggs.

RESPONSE

Gather group members in a circle around the plastic. Remove the volunteer's blindfold and ask him or her to read aloud Numbers 11:1-9. Discuss: Why did the volunteer lose perspective in the egg maze? How was this like the Jews losing perspective with Moses? What things distracted them? How can we keep focused on God's will for our lives?

CLOSING

Ask kids to each grab an edge of the plastic, walk over to a trash can and dump it. Say: Let's trash our distractions and keep focused on God! ∎

A Mirror Dimly

■ **Theme:** Understanding
■ **Scripture:** 1 Corinthians 13:12
■ **Overview:** Kids will learn that we don't understand many things today, but one day we will when God will reveal all things.
■ **Preparation:** Gather a pencil and a "What Am I?" handout for each person. You'll also need a Bible, a bag of jellybeans and some aluminum foil. Wrap the entire bag of jellybeans in foil for the last part of the devotion.

EXPERIENCE

Pass out a "What Am I?" handout and pencil to each person. Allow a few minutes for kids to guess what the dot-to-dot picture is. Say: Things are not always the way they look. Take a minute or so to try to connect the dots and see what the real picture is.

RESPONSE

After they are finished, show the sample completed drawing and talk about how the activity relates to 1 Corinthians 13:12. Explain that now we don't understand a lot of what happens in the world, but someday God will give us understanding and solve our puzzlement. Have the group members say things they'd like to know about someday. For example, how was the world created? Why did Adam and Eve allow Satan to deceive them? Will I get a chance in heaven to see my friend who died?

▨ CLOSING

Pass around the aluminum-covered surprise. Have the kids take turns guessing what it contains. Say: Right now we can only guess what's inside. When I open it you'll see clearly what it is.

Open it up and have the jellybeans for a snack. ■

What Am I?

Instructions: Connect the dots and see if you can tell what the picture is.

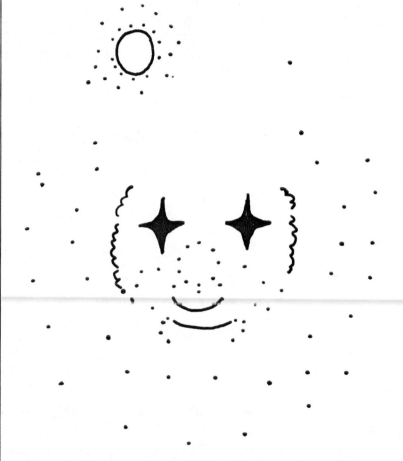

"Now we see but a poor reflection as in a mirror; then we shall see face to face. Now I know in part; then I shall know fully, even as I am fully known" (1 Corinthians 13:12).

A Rose Is a Rose

■ **Theme:** Forgiveness, sin
■ **Scripture:** Isaiah 1:18
■ **Overview:** Young people will visualize forgiveness making our sins white as snow.
■ **Preparation:** You'll need one red rose and one white rose.

EXPERIENCE

Form a circle with group members. Then pass a red rose around for them to smell. As each person holds it, encourage him or her to give a one-word description such as "pretty," "fresh," or "bright."

Read aloud Isaiah 1:18. Pass the rose around again and have each person pluck off one petal.

RESPONSE

Talk about sin and how it plucks away our self-worth and identity. Ask: How is the full, beautiful rose like how God wants us to be? How is the plucking of the rose petals similar to the way sin plucks at our lives? How can we be made "white as snow" like the Bible verse says? How does God's forgiveness make us whole?

CLOSING

Bring out a fresh, white rose. Pass it around and let everyone smell it. Say: This is what we are like when we are made "white as snow," forgiven, made new in Christ.

Display the rose in the youth room or in the church sanctuary. ■

Clean Hearts

■ **Theme:** Spiritual growth, service
■ **Scripture:** Psalm 51:10-12
■ **Overview:** Kids will design fliers to symbolize these verses and learn that God's forgiveness cleanses them for greater service.
■ **Preparation:** Gather equipment needed for cleaning car windows. You'll also need paper, markers and a Bible. Place the cleaner and rags in the center of the room.

EXPERIENCE

Gather around the window cleaning equipment. Read aloud Psalm 51:10-12 one line at a time. Have the kids repeat each line after you. Say: God's love and forgiveness clean every speck of dirt from our lives so we can shine. We're going to use these cleaning supplies you see and show others God's love. We're going to arrange a time to clean every windshield during church services when the parking lot is full of cars. When we're through, we'll place a flier under a wiper blade on each car.

RESPONSE

Give every two or three people a piece of paper and a marker. Encourage them to design a flier that symbolizes the verses you just read. For example, a flier could contain a bright, sparkling sun with the words, "Let God's love shine in your life" or "Shine for Jesus."

CLOSING

Discuss the flier creations. Decide when you want to meet to clean windshields. Choose a couple of people to make photocopies of all of the fliers. Be sure you have enough for one flier per car. ■

Commercial Break

- **Theme:** Faith, security, God's love
- **Scripture:** Psalm 23:1-6
- **Overview:** Group members will make commercials to show that everyone needs a good shepherd.
- **Preparation:** Set up four tables in the room. On each table, place some construction paper, markers, scissors, tape and a Bible. If you have the equipment and want to take the time, bring video equipment to tape the commercials.

EXPERIENCE

Send kids to tables so that each table has an equal number of people. If you have fewer than eight kids, do this together and don't divide into small groups. Instruct the groups to read Psalm 23:1-6 and create a commercial to portray the psalm's message. For example, a group could write on separate pieces of construction paper "Worried," "Lost," "Scared." One person could stand alone looking forlorn. Another person could tape the words on the person one at a time as a narrator says: "Are you worried about life? Do you feel like you've lost your way? Are you scared and all alone? You need a good shepherd to carry you through these times. You need a shepherd to guide you." Another person could come on and hug the lonely person, then help him or her off the stage.

RESPONSE

Show the commercials either by having each group act out its commercial or by using the videotaped versions.

CLOSING

Say: We interrupt our devotion for one final message.

Then reread Psalm 23:1-6. If you choose to videotape the commercials, plan a time to show them to Sunday school classes or to the congregation for a children's sermon. ∎

Follow Me

//

■ **Theme:** Commitment, spiritual growth
■ **Scripture:** Matthew 4:18-25
■ **Overview:** Kids will compare helium-filled balloons to our call to follow Christ, helping kids understand the importance of continued enthusiasm in following Christ.
■ **Preparation:** Prepare a helium-filled balloon for each person. Half of the balloons should be fresh, newly filled ones and the other half should be old, droopy ones. Gather paper, pencils, a Bible, newsprint and a marker.

◈ EXPERIENCE

Pass out one helium-filled balloon to each group member. Some have just been filled and some are old. Ask the young people to release the balloons. Some will rise and some will not. Compare this to our commitment to Christ. At first it's great, but it may dwindle with time.

◈ RESPONSE

Read aloud Matthew 4:18-25. Using the newsprint and marker, list ways the disciples showed excitement in their commitment. Discuss how we can keep our enthusiasm.

◈ CLOSING

Give everyone a piece of paper and a pencil. Have the group members each prepare an acrostic using the word "commit." Each line should be a tip for staying enthused and committed to Christ. Have kids share the acrostics when everyone is finished. Here's an example:

Care for others.
Only have eyes for God.
Make room for devotions.
Make time for worship.
In every way, serve the Lord.
Take time to pray without ceasing. ■

Follow the Leader

■ **Theme:** Commitment

■ **Scripture:** Matthew 6:24

■ **Overview:** Kids learn about stretching and building their levels of commitment after doing physical exercises.

■ **Preparation:** Ask two kids to lead exercises for the devotion. They can do jumping jacks, toe touches, stretches, and so on. Have them lead different exercises at the same time. You'll also need a Bible.

EXPERIENCE

Ask the two leaders to come to the front of the group and lead their exercises. Tell the group members to follow both leaders. Stand back and watch the confusion!

RESPONSE

Ask everyone to cool down by walking in place while you read aloud Matthew 6:24. Let the group members relax and discuss these questions: What does it mean that you can't serve two masters? What happens when you try? Why does God want us to commit our lives totally to him?

CLOSING

Have the kids form one straight line behind one leader. Instruct them to follow the leader around the room. Tell the leader to say this prayer one word at a time. After each word, have the person behind the leader say it, then the next person say it, and so on.

"God . . .
help . . .
us . . .
follow . . .
only . . .
you . . .
Amen." ■

Heavenly Grades

■ **Theme:** Spiritual growth
■ **Scripture:** Acts 2:42-47; Philippians 4:13
■ **Overview:** Kids will discover that just like we feed ourselves with new facts in school, we must continue to feed ourselves spiritually and grow.
■ **Preparation:** Gather a pencil and a "Heavenly Grades" handout for each person.

◆ EXPERIENCE

Gather the kids and say: Let's pretend this room is a grading scale. The left side of the room represents the grade A for "excellent." The right side represents the grade F for "failing." The middle represents the grade C for "average." I'll say one area of your spiritual life and you move to the part of the scale that represents the grade you feel you deserve in that area right now.

Use these areas: Bible study, quiet time, church attendance, youth group participation. After each one, allow a few minutes for kids to discuss why they've graded themselves this way.

▩ RESPONSE

Distribute a "Heavenly Grades" report card and a pencil to each person. Ask the kids to grade themselves on several areas in their present spiritual life.

Then have a volunteer read aloud Acts 2:42-47. Ask: What did the early Christians do to grow spiritually? What ideas can we get for our own spiritual growth from these verses? What role does the Spirit play in our spiritual growth?

◆ CLOSING

Have the young people complete their report cards by writing what they want to do to improve their grades. Read aloud Philippians 4:13 and discuss the comfort that verse gives. Have the kids take home their report cards as reminders to grow.

Follow up this devotion a few weeks later by giving kids another report card and asking them to grade themselves again. Have them check to see if their grades have improved. ■

Heavenly Grades

Instructions: Grade yourself in each of these areas as you feel you are right now in your life.

A=Excellent
B=Above average
C=Average
D=Below average
F=Failing

	Grade	Ways to improve
Bible study		
Quiet time		
Church attendance		
Youth group participation		
Other areas		

I Believe

■ **Theme:** Faith

■ **Scripture:** Ephesians 2:8-9; Hebrews 11:6

■ **Overview:** Group members will pantomime several situations to help them learn the meaning of faith.

■ **Preparation:** Gather several different Bible translations. Bring a plate of cookies with one cookie per person.

EXPERIENCE

Read aloud each of these situations and have all the group members pantomime together:

● Carefully sit on a chair and see how it supports you. Show surprise that it's supporting you.

● Climb a ladder and see how sturdy it is. Show wonder at the strength of the ladder.

● Plug in a radio and listen to it. Show amazement at how it works.

RESPONSE

Say: Each of the situations we pantomimed demonstrated faith. We sat on a chair and had faith it would support us. We climbed a ladder and had faith it would support us. We plugged in a radio and had faith it would work.

Ask kids to think of other situations in which they exercise faith. For example, having faith that a plane will fly.

Ask students to read aloud Ephesians 2:8-9 and Hebrews 11:6 from several translations. Then ask them how the different translations define the word faith.

CLOSING

Ask each person to define the word faith. Encourage kids to think about their faith and reread the passages every day for the next week. Hold up a plate of cookies and say: I know you have faith that I made these cookies for you.

Reward group members' faithfulness with a cookie. ■

Mouthwatering

- **Theme:** Temptation
- **Scripture:** Matthew 22:37; 26:41; 1 Corinthians 10:13; James 1:2-4
- **Overview:** Group members will have a firsthand, tempting encounter and will learn ways to resist temptation.
- **Preparation:** Gather a 3×5 card, pencil and two pieces of candy for each person. You'll also need a Bible and some clear tape.

EXPERIENCE

Pass out a piece of candy to each person and instruct the kids not to eat it. Ask four volunteers to each read one of the four scripture passages. After each passage discuss, What do we learn about temptation from these words?

RESPONSE

Pass out a 3×5 card and pencil to each person. Have kids each draw a picture of something that's really tempting to them. Discuss the temptations. Then have the kids each write the four passages on their card and tape the candy to it.

CLOSING

Tell the kids to keep their cards as reminders to read scripture daily. Remind them that God helps them deal with temptations. Then reward the kids for resisting the temptation to eat the candy by giving them each another piece of candy they can eat. ■

My Cup Overflows

■ **Theme:** Spirit-filled lives, God's love
■ **Scripture:** John 15:9-11
■ **Overview:** Group members will conduct an experiment and discover what it means to overflow with God's love.
■ **Preparation:** Gather several paper cups. Fill some with white vinegar and some with water. You will also need some baking soda and a Bible. Spread newspapers on the floor. Prepare a song for the Closing.

▦ EXPERIENCE

Divide the group into small groups of three by having kids each join hands with two others standing by them. Give each small group one cup filled with white vinegar, another cup filled with water, and some baking soda.

Say: We are all gathered here to conduct an experiment. The first event you will witness is symbolic of the life of a nonbeliever. Pour some baking soda in the cup of water. Discuss your observations.

Kids will observe that the water and baking soda do nothing. Be sure kids are standing over the newspaper. Then say: Next, continue the experiment. This event is symbolic of the life of a believer. Pour some baking soda in the cup of vinegar. Discuss your observations.

Kids will observe that the vinegar and baking soda overflow.

▦ RESPONSE

Read aloud John 15:9-11 and discuss God's love for us and what that means for our lives.

◈ CLOSING

Sing an appropriate song, such as "Bubblin' " from *Songs* (Songs and Creations), that tells of Jesus' love overflowing in our souls. ■

Shine Your Light

■ **Theme:** Witnessing

■ **Scripture:** Matthew 5:14-16

■ **Overview:** In this devotion, group members will talk about witnessing.

■ **Preparation:** Gather a Bible, one large candle, some matches and a large wicker basket. You'll also need one small candle for each person. Prepare a song for the Experience. Before the young people arrive, light the large candle and put a basket over it. Then turn out the lights. For safety reasons, you can use a large can with small holes in it.

⚉EXPERIENCE

Invite group members into the darkened room and ask a teenager to read aloud Matthew 5:14-16. The person won't be able to because it will be too dark. Don't allow anyone to turn on the lights. Tell the person to decide what to do so he or she can read. The volunteer should go closer to the basket and lift it off the candle. If he or she doesn't do this, you can.

After the candle is free from the shadow of the basket, ask someone to hand out the candles as you read aloud Matthew 5:14-16. Then have someone lead "This Little Light of Mine" from *Songs* (Songs and Creations). As the group sings, light each person's candle with the large one.

✎RESPONSE

Discuss these questions in the shining light: What does it mean to let your light shine? Why is it difficult to witness to others? What are some ways we can let our lights shine?

◈CLOSING

Have kids each blow out their candles. Say: This is what it is like if we do not share our light with others. Go and be light to a dark world. ■

Sin and Sinner

■ **Theme:** Sin, forgiveness
■ **Scripture:** John 8:2-11
■ **Overview:** Kids will experience showing their emotions about sin and forgiveness without using words.
■ **Preparation:** You'll need a Bible.

▨ EXPERIENCE

Tell everyone that you're going to have a "pantomime time" when you communicate without using sounds. Have the kids silently show you how they'd react if they:

● Smelled week-old rotting fish in a trash can.

● Walked through the sludge of mud, trash and slime in a polluted river.

● Heard that a person had committed a terribly horrifying and repulsive sin.

▨ RESPONSE

Read aloud John 8:2-11 and say: Using pantomime, show me how God would respond to you if you had committed a terrible sin. Kids could hug themselves or pat their shoulders to show forgiveness.

▨ CLOSING

Do a pantomime prayer to thank God for his love, forgiveness and acceptance, no matter how bad the sin. You say the prayer and pantomime the action, and the kids imitate your movements.

God (raise arms up and look heavenward) . . .

Help us reject the sin (shake your forefinger) . . .

But love the sinner (hug self) . . .

Thank you for forgiving us when we sin (hands folded as in praying) . . .

And loving us no matter what (hug self again) . . .

Amen (fold hands and bow head). ■

Strong Together

■ **Theme:** Forgiveness

■ **Scripture:** Genesis 13:5-9

■ **Overview:** Kids will build a human wall to help them see the importance of forgiveness and the fact that they need each other.

■ **Preparation:** You'll need a Bible.

▨ EXPERIENCE

Instruct young people to build a "human wall" by forming a pyramid or by standing side by side with arms interlocked. Ask two young people to try and knock down the wall.

◈ RESPONSE

After a few minutes of "wall busting," ask the two "wall busters" to read aloud Genesis 13:5-9. Discuss these questions: Why is there strength in numbers? How did this activity show us that we need to get along? Why did Lot, Abram and their people fail to get along?

▨ CLOSING

Ask the young people to hook arms again. Allow a few minutes of silence and ask kids to each think of someone they can't get along with. Then pray: God, give us strength to be willing to say "forgive me" to this person. Amen. ■

Unsightly Scars

■ **Theme:** Forgiveness, sin

■ **Scripture:** Acts 13:38-39

■ **Overview:** Group members will compare a scarred block of wood to sin and discuss how God's forgiveness is the only way to get rid of sin in our lives.

■ **Preparation:** Bang up and scar three pieces of wood. Drive some large nails into them and pull the nails out. Pound the wood with a hammer. Bring one good piece of wood, three pieces of sandpaper, three black markers and a Bible.

EXPERIENCE

Divide the group into three small groups by having kids sound off by spelling "S-I-N." All "S's" form one group, and so on. Give each group a scarred block of wood and a piece of sandpaper. Have the group members try to sand away the scars. They'll soon realize they can't sand away all the scratches and gouges.

RESPONSE

Give each group a black marker and have one person in each group write on its piece of wood "Sin." Ask group members to discuss how that block symbolizes sin in our lives. They will realize sin leaves a scar and nothing we do can get rid of it.

CLOSING

Bring out a fresh block of wood and ask the group members to form a circle around it. Read aloud Acts 13:38-39 and say: God has the power to wipe away all our sins. There is nothing we can do to get rid of them. God will forgive us and heal our scars if we ask him to. ■

Where the Power Is

■ **Theme:** Holy Spirit
■ **Scripture:** Acts 1:8; 1 John 1:8-9
■ **Overview:** With the use of electric power, kids will see the importance of plugging into the source of energy, the Spirit, for their spiritual lives.
■ **Preparation:** Gather two lamps, two tables, two light bulbs and a Bible. Place a lamp on each table and unscrew the light bulbs. Then plug in the lamps.

EXPERIENCE

Divide the group into two teams and assign each team a table. On the word "Go," have each team try to figure out what's wrong with their lamp and get the light to work.

RESPONSE

Gather by the light of the lamps and read aloud Acts 1:8 and 1 John 1:8-9. Say: Even though the lamps were plugged in and the power was there, they didn't work at first. Something was wrong. This is just like the Holy Spirit whose power is with us, but to have it flow through us we must get rid of anything that is wrong and confess our sin.

Ask: How do we receive the power of the Holy Spirit? Is the power available to all? Explain. Why do more people not tap into the power?

CLOSING

Turn on one lamp and unplug the other. Say: This is the way some Christians are—some are plugged into the power and some are not. What do you want for your life? ■

Worldly Blues

■ **Theme:** God's peace
■ **Scripture:** John 14:27; 16:33
■ **Overview:** Group members will discuss God's peace.
■ **Preparation:** Write the words of John 14:27 on a piece of posterboard. Gather a current newspaper, bottle of glue, pair of scissors and piece of posterboard for each small group of four people. You'll also need a Bible.

EXPERIENCE

As young people enter the room, give each one either a newspaper, bottle of glue, pair of scissors or piece of posterboard. Ask kids to form a small group by finding three people with each of the other items. If you have fewer than eight kids, simply do this devotion together.

Ask the small groups each to make a collage of pictures, articles and headlines that show the unrest of the world. After they are completed, let each small group describe its creation to the other groups.

RESPONSE

Read aloud John 14:27 and 16:33. Ask: Do we know when peace will come? Explain. Is unrest a way of life for us? Explain. How do these verses make you feel?

CLOSING

Place all the collages in the center of the room. On top of the posters, lay the posterboard with John 14:27 written on it. Gather in a circle around the posters and join hands. Have the group members each pray silently for peace in the world and God's peace in their life. After a few moments of silence, read together John 14:27 as a closing amen: "Peace I leave with you; my peace I give you. I do not give to you as the world gives. Do not let your hearts be troubled and do not be afraid." ■

10°-MINUTE DEVOTIONS for Special Occasions

I Promise to . . .

■ **Theme:** New Year's resolutions
■ **Scripture:** Ecclesiastes 5:5; Philippians 4:13
■ **Overview:** Young people make New Year's resolutions and lift them up to God.
■ **Preparation:** For each person, you'll need a helium-filled balloon with a string, a marker that will write on and not burst a balloon, paper and pencil. You will also need a Bible.

⬙EXPERIENCE

Give each person a piece of paper and a pencil. Have group members write three New Year's resolutions. Then have them prioritize the list.

Next, give each person a helium-filled balloon and a marker. Let them each list their resolutions on their balloon.

⬙RESPONSE

Discuss the resolutions. Read aloud Ecclesiastes 5:5 and ask: Why is it better not to make a promise than to make a promise and not keep it? Why are New Year's resolutions hard to keep?

Read aloud Philippians 4:13 and ask: According to this verse what resource do we have to help us keep our New Year's resolutions?

⬙CLOSING

Gather outside for a closing prayer and balloon-flying ceremony. Ask young people to keep their eyes open as you pray: God, help us keep our promises and produce long-lasting results. Keep watch over us this new year. Amen.

On "Amen," kids release their balloons as a symbolic offering to God. ■

Love Is Forever

■ **Theme:** Valentine's Day, love

■ **Scripture:** 1 Corinthians 13

■ **Overview:** Group members will learn about real love as they collect symbols for each verse of 1 Corinthians 13, the love chapter.

■ **Preparation:** You'll need a Bible and candy hearts.

▨ EXPERIENCE

Assign each person one verse of 1 Corinthians 13. If you have fewer than 13 kids attending, assign two or more verses to each person. If you have more than 13 attending, assign the same verse to more than one person. Tell kids that their task is to listen as you read the chapter and then search the surrounding area to find a symbol for their assigned verse.

Read 1 Corinthians 13, noting each verse number as you read. Give the kids a few minutes to find their symbols. For example, a person could find two pan lids to symbolize "clanging symbols" in verse one.

▨ RESPONSE

Gather the group together after kids have found their symbols. Reread the chapter, one verse at a time. Let each person explain his or her symbol.

▨ CLOSING

Pass out candy hearts and let the kids crunch on them as they chew on the facts of the devotion. Say: First Corinthians 13 tells us how we should ideally love. Let's focus on these guidelines for this Valentine's Day. ■

He Is Risen

■ **Theme:** Easter

■ **Scripture:** Luke 24:22-35

■ **Overview:** Group members will view Easter in a different light and think about "the rest of the story."

■ **Preparation:** Gather a piece of paper and a pencil for each person. You also need a Bible.

EXPERIENCE

Have group members write "the rest of the story" in this devotion. Give each person a piece of paper and a pencil. Then say: The situation is this: You lived during the time of Christ. You heard what was going on because your mother and Jesus' mother were best friends. You went with them and watched from a distance as Jesus was crucified. You watched as your mother cried for her friend. You and your mother went home. She later made some food to take to Mary and asked if you would go along with her. You did. You and Mary ended up sitting together alone in the living room while others were in the kitchen. What did you say to Mary? Write the rest of the story on your paper.

RESPONSE

Let the young people share what they've written. Before each one is read, have the kids say: "The rest of the story is . . ."

CLOSING

Read aloud Luke 24:22-35. Then say: The rest of the story is . . . Jesus lives. He died for our sins on that dark Crucifixion day, but rose again on a bright Easter. He lives. Our sins can be forgiven if we confess Christ as Lord. We'll live with him forever. ■

Who Do We Appreciate?

■ **Theme:** Mother's Day, Father's Day, parent appreciation

■ **Scripture:** Proverbs 6:20-22; Ephesians 6:1-3

■ **Overview:** Kids will prepare a videotape or cassette tape full of affirmations for their parents. The affirmations can be used later for a "Parent Show." Kids will also make cards for their parents.

■ **Preparation:** You'll need a videotape and video equipment or a cassette tape and tape recorder. Gather a piece of paper and pencil for each person. You'll also need a Bible.

EXPERIENCE

Tell the kids that during this devotion they'll prepare a videotape or a cassette tape to later play for their parents. Ask one group member to be a talk show host and conduct a group interview. Have kids take turns completing the sentence, "I love my (mother and/or father) because . . ." Videotape or record their responses.

RESPONSE

Read aloud Ephesians 6:1-3. Distribute paper and pencils and let group members each design a card for their parents telling one thing they will do to honor each of them. For example, wash the car, fix dinner or clean the kitchen.

CLOSING

Read aloud Proverbs 6:20-22. Give the kids a few minutes to each think about one thing their parents have done or said that has made an impact on their life. Videotape or record their responses as they share with the group.

Let the talk show host lead a group prayer of thanks for parents. Let everyone add a sentence or two. Stop recording now.

Plan a "Parent Show." Invite parents to view or hear the tape and receive the cards of promises. ■

Onward Toward the Goal

■ **Theme:** Graduation, spiritual growth, following Christ
■ **Scripture:** Philippians 3:13-14
■ **Overview:** Group members will race wind-up toys and discuss graduation and keeping their eyes focused on God.
■ **Preparation:** Gather a Bible and a few wind-up toys.

▦ EXPERIENCE

Divide the group into two small teams with guys against girls. Give each team a wind-up toy and have races. See whose toy is the fastest. Then see whose toy is the strongest. Create some of your own races.

▦ RESPONSE

Ask the kids to say some of the things they noticed about the wind-up toys. For example, ''As long as they're wound up, they keep moving'' or "Even when they run into a wall, they keep walking and don't change directions."

Give the group members a chance to be wind-up toys. Have them all stand up and face different directions. Then have them follow all the directions you give them and keep going even if they run into an obstacle. For example: "Take five steps straight ahead." "Walk backward 10 steps." "Walk sideways seven steps."

Discuss these questions: What are some of the plans you have after graduation? Why are clearly defined goals important? How will you know if you've hit a wall in life and need to change directions? How can God continue to guide your life?

▦ CLOSING

Read aloud Philippians 3:13-14. Offer a prayer for the graduating seniors, asking God to guide them wherever they go and whatever they do. ■

School's Out

■ Theme: Summer vacation, school holiday

■ Scripture: Psalm 34:1-3; Ephesians 6:10-17

■ Overview: Do this devotion prior to summer vacation or a school holiday. Kids will learn to keep their minds focused on God at all times.

■ Preparation: Place the following items in a suitcase: clocks, quarters, Frisbees, clothes, Bibles. Bring enough of the items to give one to every two group members.

⊞ EXPERIENCE

Bring out the suitcase and give an item to every two people. Instruct the partners to think of one or two "time-off tips" to keep their minds on God during the vacation. For example:

- Clock—Make good use of time and opportunities to read scripture daily.
- Quarter—Don't forget your offering to church even if you're on vacation.
- Frisbee—Make new friends and search out those who are lonely.
- Clothes—Clothe yourself in the armor of God (Ephesians 6:10-17).
- Bible—Keep it with you to remind you of your commitment and read it!

⊞ RESPONSE

Have each pair explain their time-off tips. As the pairs explain, have them pack their item in the suitcase.

⊞ CLOSING

Take the Bible from the suitcase and read aloud Psalm 34:1-3. Encourage the kids to keep their minds focused on God during their vacation. Place the Bible in the suitcase, close it and wish everyone a happy time off! ■

I Remember

■ **Theme:** New school year, reminiscing, looking ahead
■ **Scripture:** 1 Corinthians 9:24-27
■ **Overview:** Group members will look at past fun memories and look forward to things to come. You can use this devotion for the beginning of a school year or whenever you need to put the past to rest and look to the future.
■ **Preparation:** Bring a pair of sunglasses and a Bible.

⬦ EXPERIENCE

Gather the members in a circle and read aloud 1 Corinthians 9:24-27. Say: These verses compare the life of a Christian to that of a runner. The runner always looks ahead and keeps his or her eyes on a goal. The goal we're facing now is a new year. To ensure a good year we must look forward and not backward. We are going to participate in an activity to put the past to rest and set our sights on the future.

Have everyone in the circle share one fun memory from the past year.

⬦ RESPONSE

Say: Now that we have reminisced about last year and the fun we had, let's look forward to next year and "foresee" new, fun things to come.

Put on the sunglasses and go first. Tell a fun event or activity you foresee for the upcoming year. For example, I foresee a fun, service-filled trip to Mexico. Pass the sunglasses to the person on your right and have him or her repeat the process. Continue until everyone has participated.

⬦ CLOSING

Pass the glasses around one more time. Have each person put on the glasses and say: "Thanks, God, for the past. Help me look to the future." Have all the group members squeeze together for a group hug and shout, "Amen!" ■

Thanks-Living

■ **Theme:** Thanksgiving

■ **Scripture:** Psalm 100

■ **Overview:** Use this devotion the week prior to Thanksgiving to give kids a lesson in "thanks-living."

■ **Preparation:** Fill a basket with fresh oranges, bananas and apples. Cover the good fruit with bad fruit, such as black bananas. Cover the entire basket with clear plastic wrap. You'll also need a Bible.

▧ EXPERIENCE

Secretly choose a number between one and 20. Ask the kids to guess the number. The one who guesses closest wins the fruit and must share it with the others. As it is passed, the group members won't want the fruit and will make all kinds of sounds, such as "Yuck."

▧ RESPONSE

Read aloud Psalm 100 and focus on the fact that Thanksgiving is near. Tell the kids we should make a joyful noise and thank God in all situations. Talk about giving thanks in all situations and looking for good in all things. Take off the clear plastic and uncover the fresh fruit.

▧ CLOSING

After you offer thanks to God, allow kids to eat the good fruit. If you have time, play "Fruit Basket Upset." Have enough chairs for all but one person to sit in a circle. Tell the extra person to stand in the center. Give everyone the name of a fruit by going around the circle and saying, "Apple," "Orange," "Banana" consecutively. When you yell "Apple," all apples have to change seats, and the person in the middle tries to get an available seat. The one who doesn't get a seat goes in the middle. Do this with each fruit. When you yell "Fruit basket upset," everyone changes seats. ■

Away in a Manger

■ **Theme:** Christmas, talents
■ **Scripture:** Matthew 2:10-11; Luke 2:11-20
■ **Overview:** Kids will each have the chance to think of one of their talents and offer it as a gift to God.
■ **Preparation:** You'll need a manger or a small crib, and a doll. Set it up to look like the manger scene on the first Christmas day. Gather a piece of paper and a pencil for each person. You'll also need a Bible.

EXPERIENCE

Give group members each a piece of paper and a pencil. Encourage them each to think of one of the talents they are blessed with and draw it on their paper. A guy who's good at football could draw a football or a helmet. A student who gets good grades could draw some books or a report card with an A+ on it.

RESPONSE

Gather around the manger and read aloud Luke 2:11-20. Say: God gave us the greatest gift of all—his Son.

Ask another person to read aloud Matthew 2:10-11. Say: Just as the wise men offered gifts to the Christ child, so we will offer gifts to him. We can offer him our talents that he has blessed us with.

One at a time, have kids place their drawing in the manger and say: "I offer God my talent of _____."

CLOSING

Have a few minutes of silence and instruct kids each to think of how they can use their gift. For example, an A+ student could decide to help others who are struggling to get good grades. An athletic person could offer to take a widowed or lonely person to a sports event at school. ■

Outward Appearances

■ **Theme:** Christmas, judging others by their appearances
■ **Scripture:** 1 Samuel 16:7
■ **Overview:** Kids will view two packages and learn you can't judge a package by its cover.
■ **Preparation:** Put an old, holey, used washcloth inside a box and wrap it with beautiful paper and ribbons. Put a shiny, new radio inside another box. Wrap it with a tattered brown grocery bag and string. Buy a box of chocolate candies. Take the candies out of the box and put them in a small, brown sack. Leave the candy box empty. You will also need a Bible.

EXPERIENCE

Place both wrapped boxes in the middle of the room about five feet apart. As kids enter, have them stand by the package they'd most like to receive. Ask them why they chose the box they did. Open the boxes and show the kids what's inside.

RESPONSE

Read aloud 1 Samuel 16:7. Talk about how many people think outward apparel and appearances are the most important things in life. But God sees and knows the heart. Discuss: Why do we sometimes judge others by their appearances? Why does God look beyond the outside into the heart? Why is it difficult for us to look at the inside of people?

CLOSING

Set out the box of candy and the paper bag. Tell the group members to choose which they want for a snack. After everyone chooses, open the containers and show the contents. Hopefully, by the end of this devotion, all have caught on and chosen the paper bag filled with candy! ■

Devotion Planner

"It seems like I've used this devotion idea before. But I can't remember when . . ."

"Didn't kids really enjoy this devotion the last time I used it? Maybe it's time to adapt it again . . ."

"I think I used this idea with the junior high group. But I may have used it at the after-church fellowship. I wish I could remember . . ."

You won't have to wonder about these kinds of things if you use this handy planning worksheet. It keeps track of which devotions you've used, where you used them and how the kids received them. Whenever you use a devotion, just jot the information on the chart. Then keep it as a handy reference for the future.

	Page	Date Used	With Whom	Response/ Comments
All God's Blessings	12			
Biting Bitterness	13			
Cut the Clutter	14			
Delegate!	15			
First Things First	17			

	Page	Date Used	With Whom	Response/ Comments
Good, Bad, Rowdy	36			
Heartfelt Words	38			
Love in Action	39			
Love One Another	40			
Rumors Hurt	42			
Serve One Another	45			
Stand by a Friend	46			
Violent World	48			
A Balancing Act	50			
A Mirror Dimly	52			
A Rose Is a Rose	55			
Clean Hearts	56			

	Page	Date Used	With Whom	Response/ Comments
Worldly Blues	71			
I Promise to . . .	74			
Love Is Forever	75			
He Is Risen	76			
Who Do We Appreciate?	77			
Onward Toward the Goal	78			
School's Out	79			
I Remember	80			
Thanks-Living	81			
Away in a Manger	82			
Outward Appearances	83			

Topical Index

Scripture Index

OLD TESTAMENT

NEW TESTAMENT